Mountain Animals

Siân Smith

Raintree is an imprint of Capstone Global Library Limited, a company incorporated in England and Wales having its registered office at 7 Pilgrim Street, London, EC4V 6LB – Registered company number: 6695582

www.raintreepublishers.co.uk
myorders@raintreepublishers.co.uk

Edited by Sian Smith and Diyan Leake
Designed by Marcus Bell
Picture research by Tracy Cummins
Production by Helen McCreath
Originated by Capstone Global Library Ltd
Printed and bound in China

ISBN 978 1 406 28068 5
18 17 16 15 14
10 9 8 7 6 5 4 3 2 1

British Library Cataloguing in Publication Data
Smith, Sian.
Mountain animals. -- (Animal in their habitats)
A full catalogue record for this book is available from the British Library.

Acknowledgements
We would like to thank the following people for permission to reproduce photographs: Getty Images pp. 6 (Glowimages), 7 (Michael S. Lewis); Science Source p. 15 (Tui De Roy/Minden Pictures); Shutterstock pp. 4, 22b (jakit17), 5 (David Dohnal), 8 (erwinf), 9 (Jean-Francois Rivard), 10, 16 (Tom Reichner), 11 (Alfie Photography), 12 (Josh Schutz), 13 (Dennis Donohue), 17 (Mariusz Niedzwiedzki), 18 (Iakov Filimonov), 19 (Francois Loubser), 21 (Josh Schutz), 20a (karamysh), 20b (Smokedsalmon), 20c (Dr_Flash), 20d (Iakov Kalinin) 22a (Jean-Francois Rivard); Superstock p. 14 (Minden Pictures).

Cover photograph of a Grizzly Bear (*Ursus horribilis*) in the Rocky Mountains, Montana, USA, reproduced with permission of Getty Images (Daniel J Cox).

Back cover photograph reproduced with permission of Shutterstock (Tom Reichner).

We would like to thank Michael Bright for his invaluable help in the preparation of this book.

Every effort has been made to contact copyright holders of material reproduced in this book. Any omissions will be rectified in subsequent printings if notice is given to the publisher.

Contents

Animals in the mountains

Look at the yak.

Look at the bear.

Look at the panda.

Look at the llama.

Look at the gorilla.

pika

Look at the pika.

Look at the sheep.

Look at the wapiti.

Look at the mountain goat.

Look at the mountain lion.

Look at the salamander.

Look at the olinguito.

Look at the hare.

Look at the marmots.

Look at the condor.

Look at the vulture.

All about mountains

There are mountains all over the world. It is very cold at the top of a mountain.

Which picture shows mountains?

What am I?

I eat grass and other plants.

I have four hooves that help me walk over rocks.

I am not a sheep.

I have a woolly coat to keep me warm.

Picture glossary

 pika

 yak

Index

22

Notes for teachers and parents

Before reading

Tuning in: Talk about what a mountain is and what it is like. Why might life be difficult for animals living on mountains?

After reading

Recall and reflection: Why do many mountain animals (yak, bear, llama, panda, gorilla, mountain goat) have thick woolly coats?

Sentence knowledge: Help the child to count the number of words in each sentence.

Word knowledge (phonics): Encourage the child to point at the word *at* on any page. Sound out the phonemes in the word: *a-t*. Ask the child to sound out each letter as they point at it and then blend the sounds together to make the word *at*.

Word recognition: Challenge the child to race you to point at the word *the* on any page.

Rounding off

Sing the following song (to the tune of "For He's a Jolly Good Fellow"):

The bear went over the mountain (3 times)
To see what he could see.
And all that he could see (2 times)
Was ...
The other side of the mountain (3 times)
Was all that he could see.

Word coverage

Topic words
bear
condor
gorilla
hare
llama
marmot
mountain
mountain goat
mountain lion
olinguito
panda
pika
salamander
sheep
vulture
wapiti
yak

High-frequency words
at
in
look
the

Sentence stem
Look at the _____.

Ask children to read these words:

yak	p. 4
panda	p. 6
sheep	p. 10
marmot	p. 17